Letters
to
Graduates

Letters to Graduates

from
BILLY GRAHAM
POPE JOHN PAUL II
MADELEINE L'ENGLE
ALAN PATON

and *others*

Myrna Grant

ABINGDON PRESS
Nashville

Library of Congress Cataloging-in-Publication Data

Grant, Myrna.
    Letters to graduates / Myrna Grant.
      p. cm.
    ISBN 0-687-21563-3 (casebound : alk. paper
    1. College graduates—Religious Life. 2. Christian life—
    1960- 3. Imaginary letters. I. Title.
    BV4529.2.G72   -   1990
    248.8'34—dc20   90-38371

ISBN 13: 978-0-687-21563-8

This book is printed on recycled acid-free paper.

10 11 12 13 14 - 14 13 12 11 10
MANUFACTURED IN THE UNITED STATES OF AMERICA

—— For ——

Amanda
Jackson
Heather
Torey
Jillian

with love

— Contents —

— *Preface* —

*I*n a very real sense, the future presents each new generation with glittering promises of happiness and success and progress. Today, as young people stand ready to enter a new century, there is a sense of anticipation and mystery. Enormous global changes have taken place in the twentieth century. As the epoch draws to a dizzying close, technology shapes the world in ways unimaginable to our ancestors. Mass media beguile us with their exaltations of money, youth, and power as advantages to be sought and desired above all else: The misery and emptiness of their pursuit is a matter of twentieth-century history.

Yet within the present generation are women and men who have achieved lives of integrity and lasting richness. They know something of the wisdom that Scripture says is above that of pearls.

Wouldn't it be intriguing to know what advice they might give to people who will live their adult lives shaping this unknown new century? The brief essays that follow are a result of pursuing this question. I am deeply indebted to each contributor for the generosity of spirit that welcomed the opportunity to speak candidly to readers on the brink of adulthood.

Special thanks are due to Margaret Heindl for her encouragement, interest, and excellent typing skills.

David Aikman
Historian, Writer

Currently Time *magazine foreign affairs correspondent, Washington Bureau. He has been bureau chief in Moscow, Beijing, Jerusalem, and eastern Europe. He speaks the Russian, French, German, and Chinese languages.*

When I was a young boy, I loved to read stories about the deeds of the ancient Greeks. I was struck by how the young men of Sparta—the rival of Athens in the fifth century B.C.—steeled themselves for war. They gladly put up with great hardships to make themselves fitter and braver. Of course, I did not like the sheer militarism of Sparta, a civilization much inferior to that of the great Athens which Sparta, after a long war, nevertheless finally defeated in 404 B.C. But I admired the Spartan dedication, the contempt for comfort whenever comfort was seen as an obstacle to great achievement.

We certainly do not live today in an age of great dedication. When the history of this era of Western civilization is written, I think it will been seen that those of us living in the West luxuriated in a degree of comfort and ease hitherto reserved only for the tiniest minorities in charge of great empires. I believe it will be apparent that we lost much of our energy, our moral heart, and even our nerve, through our addiction to the comforts of life. And it seems to me now that, unless we recover our dedication and our hardiness, there may not be much of a Western civilization left in which to indulge that addiction.

So for me the great virtues, which we must recover as Christians within this civilization by the beginning of the twenty-first century, start with those of dedication and hardiness. Dedication is simple to explain: It means commitment to Christ and the kingdom of God both when afflicted by adversity and when tempted by ease.

Hardiness is harder to define. What it really means, I think, is strength of spirit, soul, and body amid difficulties and discomforts, an unwillingness to complain or give up when faced with the pains of the rough life. The great missionary explorers like St. Francis Xavier, who brought the Christian faith to Japan, or David Livingstone, who ventured into uncharted Africa, exemplified both dedication and hardiness. These men, and others like them, learned early in life what insuperable odds can be conquered by self-discipline. They understood how the body and the mind can be tempered by hardship to accomplish almost anything.

Even non-Christians have learned—or rediscovered, to be more accurate—the values of self-denial and hardship in this century. The twentieth-century Marxist revolutionaries of Russia, China, and other countries have all been men and women so caught up in their dreams of a utopian future that they have ventured not just their comfort, but their own lives, on the altar of their cause. Can it be that they have lessons to teach us Christians?

The dedication and hardiness brought forth by consistent self-discipline, of course, do not in themselves produce the Christian fruits of the Spirit named in Paul's Letter to the Galatians: love, joy, peace, patience, kindness, goodness, faithfulness, gentleness, and self-control. On the contrary, those who achieve self-discipline through sheer will-power often slip over into arrogance. Then the will to self-mastery becomes the will to master others—with ugly and cruel results. Thus seekers after dedication and hardiness must combine these virtues with two others: humility and love.

Humility has a special role to play: It protects other virtues from corrosion by pride. It ensures that God-given talents are not misused for selfish ends. When humility is present, dedication and hardiness enlist themselves willingly for every task and challenge. They do not sneer at those not yet endowed with them. And they regard no course of action as too menial for their service.

But still there is something missing, and that is love. Even great heroism and endurance can be difficult to contemplate if the motive is empty. What love does is subdue the very greatest human qualities to the very greatest divine purpose. Love—the deliberate, unselfish, active concern for others—clothes dedication and hardiness and humility with a shining garment of God-given motive. Love is the other garment for the other virtues, the aspect of the other virtues which a stranger notices first.

Can we restore to our civilization the vigor and honesty and cleanliness of true Christian commitment? I believe we can. I do not think that even the many years of ease have bred out of young people in the West the sense of excitement at hardship, adventure—even danger—in the pursuit of the highest good of God's Kingdom. And when its finest representatives are ready to take up the immense challenges of the third millennium of Christ's Kingdom, they will rediscover the guides familiar to earlier generations of Christian adventurers: dedication and hardiness, humility and love.

A. van der Bijl, Brother Andrew
Missionary Statesman

Founder in Holland, and President of Open Doors, now a world-wide missionary organization, he has given international leadership to serving the oppressed church in closed societies and in areas of the world devastated by warfare. He serves on boards of international humanitarian and human rights organizations.

*O*kay, guy, just sit there. Yes, right there, at my feet. Since I'm your dad, and you're young, and you're just facing life, and you want to avoid all the pitfalls that somehow they never warned me against. . . . You don't want to be in power and then in prison, do you? Or be famous and then be messed up in some dirty business? Or have a breakdown in morals, or suffer the breakup of your family. . . .

Come to think of it . . . Or do you want to invent the wheel—again? Or anything else that we have already invented?

No, I know, you don't want to listen to me anyway. You blame the older generation for the mess this world is in, and for the mess of your own life—and in a sense, you're right. Young people didn't produce pornography, bad films, bad books, a bad society. . . . But then of course, what did the younger generation invent? Maybe you are hoping that some day you'll strike it rich? Make a new discovery?

The authority crisis over the last couple of decades has made it hard for young people to accept advice from parents, even from the apostle Paul, the biblical prophets, even from Jesus himself. I'd like to put my advice in the form of an illustration that takes my memory back a few years.

When I close my eyes, I can still see him: There he sits in front of me, and his drooping shoulders express the frustration and discouragement that he is facing until he jumps up from his chair and shouts at me, "If only they would *let* me!"

It was in an east European country many years ago. I was counseling a young man, a dedicated follower of Jesus Christ. He was being drafted into the army. In itself, that's not so bad, you might think, in the light of your own country and situation. But in his case, it meant that he had to take an atheistic oath and swear allegiance to the force then dedicated to wiping out the Church, and at that time he was very much aware of the spiritual conflict. In the military oath, he had to state that he would fight on the side of his country to overthrow every power that resists the influence of communism.

To Gerhard, that was a thing he would not do. He loved the Lord Jesus enough to be willing to say no, but there was no way to say no—or so it seemed. We discussed several options and in the end I said to him, "Gerhard, why don't you die as a martyr for Jesus?" And it was then that he jumped up and exclaimed, "Andrew, if only they would *let* me. I would *love* to die as a martyr for Jesus, but they won't let me. They'll convict me of some political or economic crime, but they won't let me die for Jesus."

Not many young people in the world today have to stand in his shoes. Not many people of any age would willingly die for Jesus. Shallow Christianity or ignorance of the Bible, ignorance of the will of God, ignorance about one's own self—all these stand in the way of a full knowledge of God and his will. Jesus himself said that if anyone wants to do his will (John 7:27), he shall *know* it. But many young people shrug their shoulders and say, "How can we know?"

God wants to give you a key. Just think for a moment what you could do if you had the key to knowledge, the key to guidance, the key to power, the key to the very heart of God. You know such a key would open up a world in which your life would really count.

Now is the time to jump up from *your* chair and say, "It doesn't matter whether 'they' will let me. I don't want to be with those who will be 'carried to the skies on flowery beds of ease while others fight to win the prize and sail through bloody seas.' I want to become a disciple in the fullest sense of the word, so devoted to Jesus Christ that God can reveal his complete will to me, so that I can carry out his plan in this troubled world."

Yes, it takes decision. Yes, it takes perseverance. Yes, it takes a big effort. But as good Corrie ten Boom would sometimes ask when she addressed a young peoples' meeting, "Do you think you can learn anything from a person who grew up in a time when there was no radio, no television, no automobile?" She was obviously referring to herself, but then it also applied to the apostle Paul, and the other apostles, and the prophets, and Jesus. They never saw a car, they never went surfing, they never watched TV. . . . But their lives . . . oh, their lives. Can you still follow them? Imitate them? Do the same things? Live a life of service to God that he prepares you for? This kind of service is more exhilarating than anything you can imagine, more rewarding, more fulfilling, more joyful than the pursuit of any kind of happiness. This is the life to which God calls you. Listen to older people whom you respect. Read biographies of great men and women. Study the Bible. Remember: "The world has not yet seen what God can do with one man or one woman who is fully dedicated to him."

Elisabeth Elliot
Writer

She was a missionary translator of the Bible in the eastern jungles of Ecuador from 1952 to 1963. She is the widow of James Elliot, who was one of four American missionaries martyred in the jungles of Ecuador in the 1956 by the Auca Indians. She has written about these experiences as well as biographies and books on Christian discipleship.

If people back in the thirteenth century were trying to imagine what the fourteenth would be like, they could hardly have visualized the Black Death that devastated Europe. Whether the twenty-first century will be better or worse than the fourteenth or the twentieth only God knows, but isn't it a steadying, calming thing to know that he *does* know, and has already made provision for his twenty-first century children? There's no need to "go bananas" thinking about it. I'm sure of one thing: It is not going to be easier to be an earnest disciple of the Lord Jesus than it was in the first century when he called his disciples. It has never been easy. God never promised it would be. But he's in charge, he's got the whole world in his hands, and he offers us the very best if we'll just make up our minds to go his way instead of our own.

Jim Elliot, a missionary back in the mid-fifties who ended up in a river of eastern Ecuador with a wooden spear in his back, once told a friend that he didn't like that little gospel ditty, "Every day with Jesus is sweeter than the day before." He was an exuberant, outgoing, humorous man, not some kind of doomsday nut, but he said that every day with Jesus is tougher than the day before. He had found it so because he had made up his mind about one immensely important thing—he had decided not to live for himself. The verse he wrote in my college yearbook was II Timothy 2:4, "A soldier on active service will not let himself be involved in civilian affairs; he must be wholly at his commanding officer's disposal" (TEV).

It was a radical decision. I urge you to consider it. If you choose to put yourself under orders to Jesus Christ, you will find yourself at once up against cosmic powers, and superhuman forces of evil. (Ephesians 6:10-18) That's what the apostle Paul found, it's what Jim found. I guarantee it's what you'll find (remember you heard it here and don't be surprised). A man or woman who determines to be "the right stuff" for a disciple must learn, not how to avoid dying, but how to die, how to follow the Master straight through to the Cross—which is a cross, not a rose garden.

The letters that come to me from students

convince me that, in spite of the self-indulgence that seems to characterize America now, they are drawn by the idea of sacrifice, of difficulty, of high demands. One who would help people must demand something of them. Consider the demands Jesus made: Give up your right to yourself. Take up your cross. Follow. But that wasn't all Jesus offered. He said he would give rest, an easy yoke, real and lasting happiness, peace, and—if you're faithful unto death—a crown of life.

Aristotle said, "All men seek happiness—*there are no exceptions*." What differentiates you from another is where you look for your happiness. You can take your cues from the world or you can take them from Jesus. There aren't any other choices.

When the newspapers began to ask why in the world Jim Elliot and his four missionary buddies left their wives and little children and went into the territory of a people known to be killers, I thought of what that old apostle John had said: "The world and all its passionate desire will one day disappear, but the man who is following the will of God is part of the permanent and cannot die" (I John 2:17 JBP). There was the answer to the *why*. Those men had done a lot of planning and a lot more praying. The Indians had never had a chance to hear the Good News of a loving God's offer of Life. Somebody had to tell them. They lost their lives in the attempt, but as Jim had written in his diary years before, "He is no fool who gives what he cannot keep to gain what he cannot lose." That's *fulfillment*, another word for happiness. It comes not by doing your own thing but by doing Somebody else's.

The will of God is Somebody else's thing. Jim believed God had called him to Ecuador, first to the Quichua Indians and then, when the opportunity came, to the Aucas. He was thrilled. It was the dream of a lifetime to carry the Gospel to people who had never heard of Jesus. Jim never got to tell them about Jesus. The spear got to him first, but his death spoke loud and clear to a world unaccustomed to costly commitment.

The will of God will not be what you expect. It may indeed include the dream of a lifetime (it has included many of mine), but it will lead far beyond. It is much bigger, grander, more glorious than your wildest dreams. From experience (and I haven't been to *Heaven* yet!), I guarantee it. What's far more trustworthy, the Word of God guarantees it. Go for it! You'll never be sorry.

Gillian Evelyn Brentford
Viscountess

Owner and chief executive officer of her own business, she is a consultant for several others. An active Christian laywoman and public figure, she is a speaker and writer on Christian and public policy issues and is a member of numerous national councils and committees in Great Britain.

Although the world in the twenty-first century will change dramatically, the two great fundamentals of Christian life will not. The first of these is how you create and develop an ongoing relationship with Jesus Christ. One of the most difficult areas in this new century will be the proliferation of different "belief styles." Did Jesus understand computers? Does he have anything to contribute in a world dominated by the satellite and microchip? How may faith be integrated in an increasingly technological era? In an epoch of increasing pluralism, everyone will have ideas and models. What is going to be your base line? Where is the truth criterion you will use? My own experience has been that the only true base line is what the Bible teaches. It has a framework of belief for living, of meaning for your existence, that nothing else does. Also, it contains everything you need to sort out the second fundamental of your life.

The second great fundamental of life is the question of your relationships with other people. You probably anticipate a happy, fulfilling marriage, children, and good friends. The twenty-first century will conspire against your having those things. You will have to fight for them with all the faith and skill that the Almighty can give you.

It is like building a house. A house, at its most basic, has foundations, four walls, a front door, and a roof. The foundation cement is the understanding of God's love for you, because with that comes self-acceptance. God truly loves you, not for what you can do but for who you are. As you receive that love, you also love others. The basis of our relationships with others is how we view ourselves. If we have not accepted the faults and failings in ourselves, we shall not be able to accept those of others, and the very foundations of our relationship "house" will be faulty. God is unfailing love.

The front wall of your "relationship house" is the wall of love for others. The main part of that wall is the front door. The door is the Lord Jesus. He can be the Door by which people come in and out of your life. He can guide you to friends to let into the inner places of your heart.

Forgiveness is the next wall. Whatever happens

around you, the people nearest you will often need your forgiveness. Jesus was betrayed by his closest enemies, but he was also betrayed by his friends. You may sometimes feel that you have been too. Forgiveness is how he responded and what he has taught us to do.

Communication is the third wall. Love is not silent nor is forgiveness. They are spoken, touched, sensed, laughed, cried, and seen. One part of communication is prayer. Communication with our heavenly Father—our heavenly Protector, our Comforter—is a great gift. As we pray, our ability to get through in words, looks, and touches to those whom we love is greatly strengthened. Another part of communication, getting through, really making people understand you and what you are trying to say, is an art to be learned. It takes time and attention.

The back wall of your "relationship house" is the wall of trust. It is built slowly over a period of months or years. Part of the wall is built on learning the deep trustworthiness of God. Surprisingly, part of the wall will only be strong and invulnerable as you take a few risks and discover when to give trust. For example, people who do not keep your secrets are not trustworthy. You will find that those who do are worth a fortune.

The winds of rapid change and opposition will certainly batter your twenty-first-century life. You will be glad of the firm foundation of the Love of God, the roof of the Protection of the Lord Jesus Christ, and the Power of the Holy Spirit. Life will be a challenge in the 2000s, but built on strong, sure foundations of the truth of the Bible and God's love, your life will be secure and meaningful.

Donald Coggan
Former Archbishop of Canterbury

A scholar of Semitic languages and the New Testament, he was Bishop of Bradford before becoming Archbishop of York in 1961. He was appointed the Archbishop of Canterbury in 1974.

*I*n the first place, it is unlikely you will see the end of the twenty-first century. So—time is limited. Don't waste it. Don't fritter it away. Use it for making a worthwhile character. After all, that is the only thing that you will take with you when these few decades are through. You won't take your money, or any reputation you may achieve, or any books you may write. You *will* take your character. These years are preparatory years for an even fuller, richer life beyond. Use them to that end.

This is not morbid advice; it is realistic. "Aim at nothing and you will hit it." Make a strong character your goal, and you may well achieve it.

Second, find a master, someone to whom you can give your whole-hearted allegiance. That sounds as if it would lead to bondage. As a matter of fact, it is the surest road to freedom. Here is a paradox that enshrines a great truth. For the Master I have in mind is Christ. "To serve him is to reign." That service releases you from bondage to yourself—and that is a mighty release! Jesus said, "If anyone wishes to be a follower of mine, he must leave self behind." That is a clear choice. "He must take up his cross and come with me." That is costly. "Whoever cares for his own safety is lost; but if a man will let himself be lost for my sake, he will find his true self." There is the great alternative; and there is the great promise —finding your true self.

Next, find a life-work to which you can dedicate yourself with abandon. That advice is easier given than obeyed, for it may well be that many who read this chapter will be forced to face—through no fault of their own—the agony of unemployment. But many—most, we hope—will spend the major part of their lives gainfully employed. The fortunate ones are those who find themselves so fulfilled in their work that they rarely have their eyes on the clock waiting for the hour that marks the closure of the office, or on the calendar that marks the date of retirement. Their employment is their joy. Would it be rash to suggest that such employment is most likely to be found in those areas of work that lead directly, or possibly indirectly, to the betterment of society and the fuller living of its members? *People matter*—matter more than institutions. To invest one's life in the spiritual, mental, and physical welfare of men and women is to invest it in a project of inestimable value.

Just as people are more important than institutions, so is finding the right marriage partner. Again, this is advice easier given than obeyed. Nor will it apply to all. For some are so constituted that marriage is not for them. And to some will come the call for the celibate life, with all its demands to forgo the choice of marriage in order that some great aim may be fulfilled—for example, in obedience to the call of the monastic ideal or of some work that can only rightly be done under conditions where, let us say, the rearing of a family would not provide proper opportunities for the children concerned. But to most of those who read this book will fall the choice of a marriage partner—"to love and to cherish, for better for worse, for richer for poorer, in sickness and in health, till death do us part."

"He that findeth a wife or husband findeth a good thing." How right the writer of Proverbs was! The joining of two different personalities in a union that leaves room for the development of each partner's gifts and interests as well as for the sharing of common joys and concerns—physical, intellectual and spiritual—is a never-ending miracle. The creation of a home whose head is the Lord Christ and in which music and art are constituent parts of the life lived together is a miracle that makes not only for the joy of individuals but also for the stabilizing and enrichment of society.

Whether or not finding a marriage partner is for

you, keep your eye open to the needs of the world. The odds are that you who read these words are living among the "haves." Unlike millions of your fellow human beings, you can read; you have an adequate water supply; when you are hungry you can get a good meal; you have a comfortable bed waiting for you tonight; medical care is readily available; you have books and opportunities for leisure and fun. Are you quite sure that these coming decades are to be spent in such surroundings? Keep your options open. It might well be that God is calling you to share your gifts and your training with others less fortunate than yourself. In doing this, you will find a rich fulfillment.

The years in which we are living are facing us with enormous problems—and with gigantic opportunities. The inequalities of wealth and poverty, the meteoric rise of world population, illiteracy, disease, apartheid—all these can be regarded merely as present ills or future disasters. But here is another way of looking at them. They present the men and women of the twenty-first-century world with challenges to courage and initiative and dedication. They are opportunities for life investment, for pitting one's energies of mind, body, and spirit against *one* of these evils and seeing if a dent can be made in it. And if you feel tempted to ask what one individual can do in the face of problems so huge, it might be worth recalling that Thomas Edison, whose discoveries have affected most of earth's inhabitants, said: "Genius is one percent inspiration and ninety-nine percent perspiration."

Somebody said that it couldn't be done,
But he with a chuckle replied,
That maybe it couldn't, but he would be one
Who wouldn't say so till he'd tried.
So he buckled right in with the trace of a grin
On his face; if he worried he hid it.
He started to sing as he tackled the thing
That couldn't be done, and he did it.

Somebody scoffed: "Oh, you'll never do that,
At least no one ever has done it."
And he took off his coat and he took off his hat,
And the first thing we knew he'd begun it.
With a lift of his chin and a bit of a grin,
Without any doubting or quiddit,
He started to sing as he tackled the thing
That couldn't be done, and he did it.

There are thousands to tell you it cannot be done,
There are thousands to prophesy failure,
There are thousands to point out to you, one by one,
The dangers that are sure to assail you.

But just buckle in with a bit of a grin,
Then take off your coat and go to it.
Just start in to sing as you tackle the thing
That "cannot be done," and you'll do it.

Poor poetry? Of course. But isn't there in it just that
fragment of truth that can make all the difference
between a life that achieves something noble and an
existence that benefits no one?

Perhaps G. A. Studdert-Kennedy, the famous padre of World War I, said it better:

> I bet my life
> Upon one side in life's great war. I must.
> I can't stand out. I must take sides. The man
> Who is neutral in this fight is not
> A man. He's bulk and body without breath. . . .
> I want to live, live out, not wobble through
> My life somehow, and then into the dark.
> I must have God. This life's too dull without.
> Too dull for aught but suicide. . . .
> I can't stand shivering on the bank. I plunge
> Head first.

Charles Colson
President, Prison Fellowship

Formerly special counsel to President Richard Nixon, he became a Christian in the aftermath of Watergate. He spent time in prison for his Watergate activities. Following his release he founded Prison Fellowship, today the largest evangelical outreach into prisons in America and in other countries. His Christian books have been best sellers.

W hen I first became a Christian I decided I'd better take a look at the Bible. I am a lawyer by profession. I picked up that Bible and thought I'd better read it and figure out what's in it. It says it's the Word of God. Could it really be? I read it three times from cover to cover. Actually I was looking for the one verse of Scripture that I'd always known all my life by heart. The only one, as a matter of fact. You know—the one that says, "God helps those who help themselves." The amazing thing was that I couldn't find it. I tried two different versions of the Bible to see if I could find it. I discovered, as a matter of fact, that the Bible says something quite the opposite. It says God helps those who can't help themselves. "Is this not what it means to know me—to plead the cause of the afflicted and the needy?" So I made an amazing discovery as I started to read all the evidence I could find about all the archaeological discoveries and the Dead Sea Scrolls, and I began to read about how the prophecies had been fulfilled. I came to see that the Bible is not just a book of old fables and legends and tales and ancient parables—it is a book of truth. It is the inerrant revelation of God himself, and so we first have to be discerning and then we have to have the courage to say, "I am going to take that Bible, I am going to absorb it; I am going to live under its authority; and I am going to believe it." And let me tell you something. Don't you dare go out and hang your head in the face of secular intellectuals who will say to you, "You don't really believe in that Bible, do you?" You stand right up to them and say, "I certainly do," and challenge them because the evidence is there that supports that the Bible is true, that Jesus was in fact historic. The truth of his resurrection is absolutely overwhelming. So never turn away from him. But I warn you when you start reading that book it's going to have an impact on your life.

The central covenant of Scripture, I believe, and I hope I am not treading on anyone's toes theologically, was given by God to Moses when he said, "You shall be holy because I am holy." A holy God has come to pitch his tent, to dwell in the midst of the Jews, his people, and then through the person of Christ he has come to dwell in us. And because he is holy we are to be holy.

Mother Teresa says holiness is acceptance of the will of God. I love that. John Wesley, one of the models of my life, once said that there is no holiness but social holiness. To turn Christianity into a solitary religion is to destroy it. You see, it was Wesley's understanding that we are to be instruments of justice and righteousness. A nation that would sell the poor for a pair of shoes will stand in God's judgment. We are to have compassion; we are to pursue justice for all people. Wesley understood that. That's why he wrote the first book against the slave trade in 1774.

God's word commands you to go out and be instruments of God's holiness and justice in the world around you. Don't put your blinders on. See the need and meet it. Be instruments of holiness and righteousness and justice in society. As Christians we're called not only to believe but to repent. That means to be changed. That means to live different lives.

Affluent Christianity would say God saved me, and now I'll live a saved life. I'll be smiling and singing in the choir and having a wonderful time and be respected by everybody else. God says you're going to pay; you're going to be different; you're going to repent. It may cost you a great deal.

Dietrich Bonhoeffer, the great German pastor, the martyr, went back to be with his people. He went into a concentration camp, and he died. He paid with his life because he stood against sin. I guarantee you that you're going to face hard choices, and if you do not *face* those choices, get on your knees and check your

Christian commitment, because there is something wrong. It's inevitable. If each of us doesn't choose obedience, Christians are just going to be homogenized and blended into the culture and become just part of the act. John Wesley once wrote that making an open stand against all ungodliness and unrighteousness is one of the noblest ways of confessing Christ.

Be radical. Dare to be different. Dare to be Christian. Go to the world. Accept Jesus Christ, and live for him in this affluent culture. I dare you to do it. There isn't anything else; believe me. I've tried it all. There *is* nothing else. And be determined in your own minds that whatever you're going to do, you are going to pursue it to the glory of God and make it different for him in an age that glories in what the Scriptures call sin. So gird your minds for action. Keep sober in spirit. Fix your hopes completely on the grace to be brought to you at the revelation of Jesus Christ. As obedient children do not be conformed to the former lust which was yours in ignorance, but be like the Holy One who calls you. Be holy yourselves in all your behavior. It is written, "You shall be holy because I am holy." Let it be your choice to live that radical message in the world today.

From a commencement address at Taylor University, May 18, 1985.

Jacques Ellul
Law and History Professor, Theologian

During World War II he was an active member of the French Underground Resistance and later served with distinction as Mayor of Bordeaux. In 1946 he joined the faculty of the University of Bordeaux. He has been highly honored by the French government and the French Academy. He is a prolific scholarly and Christian writer, and he is considered a foremost Christian thinker. He is a member of the Reformed Church.

I have few illusions on the subject on which I am going to write. Experience has taught me that the wisdom of the "ancients" is no longer heeded by the young. Yet it may be that the new generation will be different from the one that preceded it. Perhaps, like past generations, young people will once again be ready to hear the word of experience and the counsel of the past! In my opinion, there are four propositions, suggestions, observations to be considered, but I do not presume to exhaust all that could be useful to a young person today.

My first fundamental observation, decisive for all the others, is that of cultivating a critical spirit. Do not be negative, but always be alert, have your eyes constantly open, and know that no proposition, no program, no philosophy, no religion should be accepted without being first subjected to scrutiny. Therefore, we must begin by saying, "No," not as a refusal to hear or examine things, but as a refusal to adhere to beliefs without having first understood, examined, evaluated, and judged them on the basis of knowledge and experience. A critical spirit always rejects what is fashionable. Listening to a certain type of music or wearing certain clothes, because everyone does it, represents weakness and resignation. One must begin by analyzing and knowing where something will lead, and what it involves. One must be a nonconformist in large and small things (but let us keep in mind that in our relationships with society there are no small things—it is as much a mistake to drink a soda without thinking about what we are doing as it is to vote republican or democrat). I must be nonconformist not to shock my friends, not to act superior to them, but because it is the only way to become myself. It is therefore necessary to keep a cool head, that is, never to allow oneself to be overtaken by unreflected passion, be it political, social, artistic, or collective. I must consider first what is involved and then, if the cause is good, give myself wholeheartedly to it, with complete enthusiasm, once the initial seduction has left, once it is finished and scrutinized. It is not sufficient to obey the evidence. No "evidence" should make us act: We must analyze what is evident and bring it to the realm of the comprehensible and the living. In giving this counsel I draw inspiration from biblical texts as well: Paul in the Epistle to the Romans tells us: "And do not be conformed to this world, but be transformed by the renewing of your mind" (12:1-3). On the other side of the issue of testing the evidence is the text concerning the temptation of Eve. After the serpent had shown her the tree of knowledge of Good and Evil, Eve "saw with evidence" that the fruit of this tree was good to eat, pleasant to the sight, and useful for opening the mind! If she had had a critical spirit, she would have first considered *who* was suggesting that to her, *why* he was doing so, and especially *what* he was ultimately by proposing to her (to become like God), and then she would have refused in spite of the evidence!

Coming immediately after the critical spirit, I recommend the application of a principle that I formulated more than twenty years ago, which subsequently spread around: It is necessary to "think globally and to act locally," which is just the opposite of what is generally done! Often we do not try to think globally because it is long and difficult, and it seems useless. On the other hand, when we "act globally" we will say that it is pointless to help a poor man who is hungry and that what is needed is to change the political and economic systems that produce the poor! Thus we give no attention to the need at hand, being absorbed only with endeavors far removed in time and space. In the realm of reflection, knowledge, and thinking we are content with the commonplace, with information from the media, with social trends. We should proceed in exactly the opposite direction. We must think on our own, trying to make an original effort at getting the information by placing the question in its economic, historical, and other contexts. This will show us that large global undertakings are deceiving and illusory. If you wish to act on poverty, begin by helping the poor that you meet. As for the poor of the Third World, begin by informing yourself about their needs, about the possibility of getting them suitable help, but you must consider the negative effects of many humanitarian actions. All this is not to get you discouraged, but to avoid living with illusions and falling in the traps open to you. The same holds true for ecological actions. Focus on your action, your country, your city, your landscape, not on great projects, which are quickly politicized. But conversely, try to know *perfectly well* the true causes of pollution, the true dangers to be avoided, without contenting yourself with slogans. A global perspective is one that refuses ahead of time to adhere to programs, and that puts into relationship the spiritual and the economic, the social or the political. For, humanity is a *whole,* which must not be divided and which assumes that all aspects that concern humanity must be considered. Finally, the great political transformations always began with general, global thinking, which at the inception was expressed in individual actions. The great defect of current political or social movements is that they are launched with tremendous resources and large human gatherings, but without any true founding principle.

The third piece of advice that I would offer is two-fold and derives from what I have just said. Its first aspect is that we must not believe in political action and in the possibility of truly changing something by way of politics! In our world, the latter is a false pretense. Politicians in general obey the "force of circumstances." Global technological and economic systems are so powerful that nothing can be changed through political means. The politician in every country is an actor who occupies the foreground of the stage and attracts the attention of the crowds while serious things occur behind his back without the citizens' being able to really see what is going on. It is more important to try to change a certain social relationship, or even more important, the spiritual life of humanity. Politics has no effectiveness whatsoever and its rule is over. It can, of course, modify the interest rate or a police order, but it can neither stop the course of armaments, nor modify the state of the Third World, nor really help those who are poor. Concrete problems have to be approached from a more profound level than politics, that is, the spiritual being of humanity. Yet there is a contradiction between the two orientations, for there is no "Christian politics" conceivable or achievable.

The other side of this reflection or meditation concerns the poor. The young—young Christians especially—feel inclined to help the poor, to take the side of the poor. But here again serious reflection must be given, and the question must be asked: Who are really poor? The answer appears to be evident, yet it is not! The poor in contemporary society are undoubtedly still the ones who are hungry, stripped, and dispossessed of their goods, but very often when we are told of the poor located thousands of miles from us, it is a trap and a false pretense. For there are other poor who eat to their satisfaction and lack for nothing but are in fact poor. They are poor because they are threatened by powerful neighbors or isolated in the world. This is very important and counts a great deal today in the political judgments that we make. We take sides with those who are obviously poor. But such a question has to be envisioned *globally*. When we take sides we have to know exactly why and with justifiable reasons. We must not be swept away by our passions!

Finally, the last counsel that I would give is to keep contact with the past! Our society pretends that it is oriented toward the future. Only scientific and technical training really counts because that is what prepares us to enter a society of the future. But I believe that this is a grave error. A civilization, a culture exists only as a product of history; it is a slow creation, produced by many generations. A culture is not invented like a new motor! But without civilization, we will return to a primitive state even if we are brilliant engineers. In order to belong to a civilization, it is necessary to know the foundation of that civilization, its morality, its myths, and its history, that is to say its past. We must not assume that we can invent a "technical culture" as some claim to be doing. There is no technical culture because culture cannot be fabricated voluntarily or willfully in a few years. It is a complex whole that a people build upon through successive generations. And I believe that technology with its constant change, its incessant "progress," is not able to be assimilated by a culture, and is incapable of producing one. If we want to be civilized and not barbarous, we must enter into the history of one's nation, into its practices developed over the course of time, into a certain morality, a certain type of human relations. Of course, this reference to the past, this grounding or rooting into the past does not imply a rejection of the future and the changing of society! Quite the contrary! But it implies that one does not accept just any type of future, that one *judges* progress and tries to build civilization on the efforts of past generations by studying their motivations. There is no more absurd formula than tabula rasa: "Let us start with a clean slate," for this is impossible. Even when we flatly reject the past, we always end up being reclaimed by it. We cannot get rid of our historical past any more than an individual can get rid of chromosomes. The new cannot emerge and survive unless it is grounded in the past. Two possibilities are then open to us. We can refuse to take the past into consideration, hence a crisis will appear in the course of which all new developments will be destroyed, and the past will reappear more "savage" than before.

However, an alternative remains open to us: We can choose to remain grounded in the past of this civilization, and the innovations that we undertake will have all the necessary chances for success. To know history well is the best means of preparing innovations for integration into the culture.

Translated by Maria Mocuta, Foreign Language Department, Wheaton College, Wheaton, Illinois 60187.

Colleen Townsend Evans
Churchwoman, Writer

She is the author of eight best-selling books on Christian living. Her life and ministry with her husband, the Reverend Louis Evans, Jr. of the National Presbyterian Church in Washington is characterized by untiring service to the poor. She serves on boards of international organizations for world needs. In 1986 she was named Religious Heritage of America Churchwoman of the Year.

*M*y soul does not find itself unless it acts. Therefore it must act." As an almost hopeless activist I naturally resonate to these words of Thomas Merton.

The issues that most concern me—hunger, urban problems, the suffering people of our world—determine the focus of my activities. However, in recent years I have been made freshly aware that my soul needs more than activity, and must not project itself entirely in the outward direction. "The soul that throws itself outdoors in order to find itself in the effects of its own work is like a fire that has no desire to burn but seeks only to go up in smoke" (*No Man Is an Island,* Thomas Merton). The *doing* is necessary, as I see it, but the *being* is absolutely crucial, and being means time . . . quiet, unpressured, nurturing time.

Feeling this need for time to *be* in my own life, one recent morning I decided to spend a quiet day in the tiny garden of our city row house. I scooped up leaves, and, kneeling alongside the postage-stamp flower bed, I prepared the plants for their quiet fallow season as winter approached.

I'm not much of a gardener, but as I worked with the good smelling earth (asking myself why I didn't do this more often), pulling out weeds, carefully removing broken branches, it hit me. The plants can no more pull their own weeds, remove their own broken branches, or tend to watering themselves when dry, than I can supply the inner needs of my own soul from my own resources.

Leaning back on my heels to survey what I'd done to make the flower bed a thing of beauty again, instead of an eyesore filled with scraggly growth, I thought of the unkempt areas of my life—particularly my need to give God time to nurture and tend my inner life, so that my outward activities would reflect and honor him.

Leaning on my elbows and lifting my face to the sky, I felt the warm October sun as it was filtered through the bushes and our one treasured cherry tree above. As I looked upward I saw green boughs, lacy bushes, and some branches already winter-bare. And I thought of how much the length of time required for the dormant period varies from one species to the next. One may require a few weeks, another months, still another a whole winter—some may even require a dormant period of several years. Surely this variation applies to those of us in the Body of Christ as well, I thought. Not all of us have the same rate of growth, or capacity for activity; each of us has our own built-in timer. Some young Christians seem ready to shoulder a greater amount of responsibility sooner than others. We are all unique and answer to God directly, not to any man-made formula.

Thinking of the way I sometimes push myself (or *allow* myself to *be* pushed) into frantic activity, I wonder if we as a Church do not do this on a wholesale scale to the people who come into our fellowship eager and fresh. Our tendency is often to exploit new Christians, particularly if they are leaders in the community or persons in public life. It's alarming how secular we, the Body of Christ, can be in regard to people of prestige and power—embarrassingly eager to list their accomplishments, to praise *them* rather than their Maker.

I saw this in Hollywood when well-known people in the entertainment world had genuine encounters with Christ. Seldom were they given opportunity to grow in faith before they were thrust up-front to "show and tell."

It happens in Washington too with public figures of a different sort . . . and I'm convinced that being put into a "Christian celebrity" mold by well-intentioned people can disillusion these new pilgrims. They can experience a real spiritual setback before they have walked more than a few steps down the road of their new life.

A new branch cannot bear fruit until it is strong enough to bear its weight. If given too much to carry—too soon—it breaks.

Not only are new Christians exploited by being honored for who they are rather than for whom they serve, but it also happens to those mature in ministry as well. Non-stop meetings, conferences, speaking trips, too much activity, too little fallow time for growth. More often than not, this is the life-style of men and women in ministry today. But no matter how we are pushed and pulled to do too much, it must be said that the ultimate responsibility for correcting this imbalance lies squarely with us.

The temptation in ministry to try and be all things and in all places can be heady wine and must be resisted. For if we let busy work—no matter how noble—consume our lives, we can shut out God by not allowing him the time to nurture our souls and make us the people he wants us to be.

So, what is it I want to say to young people today? Something it has taken me years to learn. Slow down—make time in your life to worship and enjoy God . . . to live your life richly and fully *in him*.

Jesus called it *abiding*.

After my quiet morning in the garden, I was freshly and powerfully reminded that abiding is meant to be first in our lives, and as we abide in him, we will have so much more of value to share with the people we are to serve. Abiding is worth whatever it costs us in time, for as we abide the *being* and the *doing* are linked in a holy, healthy partnership that honors Christ. And that—after all is said and done—is what real living is all about.

William Franklin (Billy) Graham
Evangelist

His ministry as a world-famous evangelist has spanned four decades with mass crusades held throughout the world. He is the author of fourteen books and has received many distinguished honors. Since 1955 his name has appeared every year on the Gallup Poll's "Ten Most Admired Men in the World."

*D*uring my many years as a traveling clergyman to sixty-four countries I've interacted with young people around the world. In addition to the thousands who have come to our public meetings, I have given lectures at many universities from Cambridge to Harvard. I have talked personally with teenagers around the world. In spite of their diverse backgrounds, they share two common characteristics: first, a deep hunger to know God in a very real, personal way; second, an intense desire to change their world for the better. Many of the great spiritual and social reform movements of history have begun among young people.

The decisions you make during your childhood and teenage years will set the direction of your life. And no one, *no one*, can estimate the impact of your commitment to accept Jesus Christ as Savior and to follow him as Lord. I made my decision for Christ when I was sixteen. Since that day, my life has been one surprise after another of seeing God open doors of service and opportunity, far beyond anything I could have ever imagined.

I have always believed that young people are the most powerful force in the world. At no time in history has that been more true than today. In Africa, Asia, Europe, Australia, and the Americas, a new generation is emerging that can lead the world back from the nuclear precipice toward peace in Christ or push it the last few steps over the edge toward unthinkable disaster. The choices you are making right now will determine the future of your life and your world. Every choice is important, no matter how young you are or how insignificant you may feel.

When Harvard psychiatrist Robert Coles first met Ruby, he was sure she was only days or weeks away from a psychiatric collapse. He was convinced she could not endure what was happening to her without coming apart at the emotional seams. But he was wrong.

Ruby was a six-year-old black student at a New Orleans elementary school. A federal judge had just ordered the school desegregated, and the white parents were enraged. Every day, Ruby was escorted to school by fifty armed federal marshals. Every day, the white parents shouted jeers, curses, and threats at Ruby as she walked past them into the school.

Dr. Coles had gone to New Orleans in the early 1960s to help children like Ruby cope with the social upheaval and violence in their lives. He talked with Ruby many times and worried over her mental health. He waited for weeks and then months, but the expected breakdown never came.

Instead, Dr. Coles discovered that Ruby had never really been angry or scared. She had been too busy praying for the people attacking her. Three times a day she prayed for them, because, as she told Dr. Coles, "they don't know what they are doing."

After encouraging Ruby and many other "children of crisis," Dr. Coles concluded that the children we sometimes call "culturally disadvantaged" often have a greater moral sensibility than their counterparts from more affluent families and more stable environments. In fact, Coles has suggested that the truly "disadvantaged" people in the world today are the children who come from well-off, secure families, but who have no moral purpose, no sharing with others, no concern for people outside their own little world.

Through the influence of a great aunt, Ruby had been "delivered" from the forest fire of anger and hatred that almost burned out of control across America during the 1960s. The challenge she met and mastered is the very one you face as a young person today—the challenge to transcend the generation of which you are a product and a part.

One of the greatest commendations recorded in the Bible is found in Acts 13:36, "David . . . served

God's purpose in his own generation" (NIV). In order to do that, David had to rise above the mediocrity and materialism that satisfied his peers and give himself in uncommon commitment to God. Because he did just that, we remember him today as "a man after God's own heart."

In the Bible we first encounter David as a young man of exceptional courage when he killed Goliath in full view of two entire armies. But he began his rise to greatness long before when no one was watching. He was tending his father's sheep on the lonely Judean hillsides. He had long hours and low pay along with a healthy dose of obscurity. But during those monotonous days and nights, David was learning to know God in a personal way. He was also making choices based on the power and faithfulness of God.

Later, his confident statement to the cowardly and inept King Saul reflected the faith-building experiences of those days: "When a lion or a bear came and carried off a sheep from the flock, I went after it, struck it and rescued the sheep from its mouth. . . . The Lord who delivered me from the paw of the lion and the paw of the bear will deliver me from the hand of this Philistine" (I Samuel 17:34-37, NIV).

By the time of his encounter with Goliath, David had already broken free from the forces of moral and spiritual inertia that had immobilized everyone from armor bearers to generals in the forces of the Living God. David was too young to join the army, but he was able to lead by example.

A few years ago, a psychologist, Dr. William Maston, conducted a survey of three thousand people in which he asked, "What are you doing with your life?" Nearly 90 percent replied, in effect, that they were waiting for a particular event to occur—waiting to finish school, waiting to leave home, waiting to get married.

When you are in school, it's easy to think that what you do every day doesn't count for much. But it does. You are already becoming the man or woman you will be for the rest of your life. The decisions you make in your later years are no more important than the choices of attitude and behavior you are making now. The great opportunities of your life are not somewhere out in front of you, but now.

The Bible says, "Remember your Creator in the days of your youth" (Ecclesiastes 12:1, NIV). Scripture also reminds us that there is no minimum age requirement for leadership by example. "Don't let anyone look down on you because you are young, but set an example for the believers in speech, in life, in love, in faith, and in purity" (I Timothy 4:12, NIV).

The terms "righteousness" and "holiness" have often been ridiculed by young people today. They are usually associated with self-righteousness and holier-than-thou-ness, which should rightly be rejected. But true righteousness and holiness are qualities of God himself which have most perfectly been demonstrated in the person of Jesus Christ. To be holy is to be set apart for the purpose of God just as Jesus was, just as

David was, just as you must be if you are to lead and serve your generation for God.

During my life, I have known a number of people who have risen above the commonplace to lead by example and to serve the purpose of God among their generation.

How were they able to do it? They were men and women who met God in daily fellowship through the Bible and prayer. Through consistent study of the Word, they began to see things from God's point of view. Through daily, earnest prayer, the flame of God was placed in their hearts. Their motivation for service was not from outward duty or constraint, but from a burning desire within them to please God.

Serving God's purpose in your own generation is your greatest challenge as a Christian young person today. For whom are you going to live? For yourself or God? What will your generation say of you? That you had a good time? That you were successful? That you grabbed for all you could on your one-way trip through life? Or will someone record of you the simple but profound fact that you served the purpose of God in your generation? It will depend not on how you handle crises, but on the choices you make in the seemingly insignificant events of everyday life.

The great missionary educator, Oswald Chambers, said, "The test of a man's religious life and character is not what he does in the exceptional moments of life, but what he does in the ordinary times, when there is nothing tremendous or exciting on. The worth of a man is revealed in his attitude to ordinary things when he is not before the footlights" (*My Utmost for His Highest*).

May you be one young person who will break the bonds of the commonplace to serve the purpose of God in your generation.

Mark Hatfield
United States Senator

He was elected to the United States Senate in 1966. He is widely known as a champion of fiscal responsibility, human rights, and individual freedom. He has been called "the conscience" of the Senate and a "global visionary." He is the author of three books, and co-author of several others.

*M*any of the challenges that faced our world at the beginning of the twentieth century have been met and now stand as monuments of achievement. In 1900 America still was in the horse-and-buggy age, even though the railroads were expanding rapidly, inventors were experimenting with the "horseless carriage," and Orville and Wilbur Wright were ready to launch the first successful flight. Today, dramatic advances in transportation have provided rapid mobility for our society.

Breakthroughs in medical science have increased life expectancy by over twenty-seven years since 1900. Fatal diseases such as smallpox, tuberculosis, and polio virtually have been eliminated. More recently, advances in medical technology have greatly reduced the deaths associated with coronary disease. Developments such as organ transplants, artificial limbs, and advanced drugs have enhanced the quality and extended the longevity of life in the twentieth century.

Other advances in technology, agriculture, telecommunications, and computers also have marked significant achievements in this century. Coupled with political and economic stability, these advances have enabled our nation to enjoy one of the highest standards of living in the world.

In spite of these impressive achievements the central challenge of this century, and of all ages for that matter, has been ignored. The call to seek first the living God, the God of Creation, has been disregarded. We have declared our independence from God and worshiped our monuments of achievements. We have tucked him neatly away in our religious file drawer and placed our faith in humanity's created tools of power: education, technology, military might, wealth, and political institutions. As Abraham Lincoln observed:

> Intoxicated with unbroken success, we have become too self-sufficient to feel the necessity of redeeming and preserving grace, too proud to pray to the God that made us. . . . We have vainly imagined that all these blessings were produced by some superior virtue and wisdom of our own.

What have these gods of our age wrought? Have they ushered humankind into a state of utopia, of perfection? Has the humanist philosophy declaring independence from the living God brought reconciliation and peace to our world?

Despite the twentieth century's dramatic rise in education among the world community, growth in the standard of living, and the buildup of the largest military arsenals in history, the world today is riddled with tension and war. The century is marked by a rising level of violence compared with the two preceding centuries.

The wars of the twentieth century have been far more deadly and destructive than were any in the past. We have perfected the art of brutality and created weapons with enough destructive power to place us at the brink of world destruction. Terrorist incidents around the world have increased dramatically. Violent crime in America continues to rise.

Even when considering our most positive achievements of the century, we see a corrupting influence at work. Advancements in life-enhancing technology that have expanded life expectancy are tarnished by our preoccupation with life-destroying technology. Expenditures for military research far exceed expenditures for medical research. New medical discoveries extending life expectancy also have provided the tools of the abortionists.

Concurrent with our declaration of independence from God, we also have adopted independence from others. Contrary to the created order we have elevated the importance of the individual, and worshiped the god of self. The 1970s commonly are referred to as the "me decade," a time of self-actualization and fulfillment. However, as Dostoevsky observed, "Man's fundamental urge is not self-interest in the sense of conduct which will benefit oneself, but self-interest in the sense of asserting oneself, irrespective of benefit or disadvantage. Self at all costs." As a result, relationships are fragmented and people are lonely and despairing. The United States has the distinction of having the highest divorce rate in the world. Half the marriages performed each year will end in divorce.

One-third of U.S. children do not live with both parents. A survey on children living in single-parent households found that a third never saw their father, about a quarter had contact with him less than once a month and only a quarter had contact with their father at least once a week. Child abuse and neglect are reported with astounding frequency. Most alarming has been a three hundred percent rise in teenage suicide over the past thirty years.

Drug abuse continues to impact the lives of millions of Americans. The National Clearinghouse on Alcohol Information reports that approximately 18 million adults in the U.S. abuse alcohol.

D. R. Davies observed: "The prophet of secular science, the late H. G. Wells, taught that the unhindered application of scientific research would automatically bring paradise on earth. But it hasn't. It is turning the world into a hell." The evidence is clear. Humanity's created gods have not provided the reconciliation and peace that the human spirit longs for, and faith in them is, in the words of the writer of Ecclesiastes, "vanity and a striving after wind" (2:26). As a result, a spirit of hopelessness has descended upon our world.

Amid this atmosphere of despair, the God of creation proclaims to humanity a message of hope. Repentance and faith in the living incarnate Christ sweep away the shroud of hopelessness wrought by the lifeless gods of our secular age and bring reconciliation and peace. True peace, in the midst of a fragmented, tense, and violent world, is found through the redeeming work of the living God in Jesus Christ.

The Bible is replete with this theme of peace through repentance. The prophets of the Old Testament echoed God's repeated call to the people of Israel to turn from their complacency and idol worship and toward the living God. John the Baptist burst upon his contemporary scene and broke the comfortable humanism of the day with an individual call to repentance.

Following John the Baptist, Christ confronted the world with the embodiment of God's call to repentance and faith through his life, death, and resurrection. By his earthly life, he proclaimed, in word and in deed, the gospel of God. He repudiated the self-righteousness and legalism of the religious community and exposed its hypocrisy and lust for power. Renouncing civil religion the incarnate God challenged all to repent and "seek first his kingdom and his righteousness." By his death and resurrection, Christ secured the means of redemption for those who believe.

Each of us is confronted with the temptation to place our faith in humanity's monuments of achievements. While science, education, wealth, or political power may offer momentary hope and security, as a foundation they are faulty and eventually will crumble. D. R. Davies, in *The World We Have Forgotten*, captures the point beautifully:

> A Christianity which pins its hope on this world is no longer New Testament Christianity. It is a Christianity gone corrupt, and subject to the dissolving processes of time and sin. . . . The way out offered by the Gospel of Christ is a way of escape from personal bitterness, frustration, and futility which are consequent upon trust and confidence in this world.

God's call to repentance requires the rejection of faith in the created devices of human beings and the embracing of faith in Christ. Only through faith in Christ can we experience the redeeming effects of his grace in our lives and become agents of his reconciling love throughout the world.

Madeleine L'Engle
Writer

She has received many celebrated awards for her novels. In 1963 she received the Newbury Medal for her children's book, A Wrinkle in Time. *She is a popular speaker and teacher at writing conferences throughout the world.*

What advice would I give a young person as he or she looks forward to adulthood? Well, by far the best piece of advice any of us can give is ourselves—if we are creative, open, joyous adults, then adulthood is to be rejoiced in, not shunned. If I am not a mature adult, no one is going to be able to hear anything I say.

If the young questioner is responsive and able to listen, then I would urge growing up into an open and not a closed universe. I would urge an eagerness to ask questions, which leads to new questions. If we are honest in our faith, then we need never fear questions. I would urge that we human beings try to grow spiritually as far as we have grown intellectually. Right now there is a terrible chasm between the two, which needs to be narrowed if we are to survive as human beings. We should not be afraid to let our understanding of God and of Christ deepen and widen and stretch. This begins at home, with each one of us. Being judgmental of others is mean-spirited and closes off our own ability to grow. It is hard not to be judgmental about those who are judgmental, but we have to try!

So, I would urge the courage to ask the difficult questions that have no finite answers; the courage to be joyous and vulnerable and alive; the courage to dare, to take risks; the courage to love where loving is not easy; the courage to accept our own selves, just as we are, as children of God, loved without qualification.

One young reader asked me in a letter how she could remain a child all her life and never grow up. And I replied that she couldn't, and that it would not be a good idea if she could. But what she could do, and what I hoped she would do, was to remain a child all her life *and* grow up. So I would urge the young questioner never to lose the child within—the eager, open, questioning child, able to rejoice in all the excitement of God's world, to play, to laugh.

But most of all I think that we who are "grown up" should be willing to be examples, or, as today's jargon has it, "role models." That means we have to be willing to stick out our necks and be vulnerable and open, to forgo the clichés of easy answers. There aren't any. God promises us love, promises to be with us no matter what happens, but does not promise to spare us from illness and accident and death. The wicked flourish, and the innocent suffer, and nobody has been able to explain why we've made such a mess of God's extraordinary gift of free will. We are all suffering from our abuse of the beautiful planet given us to care for; we have polluted air, water, land. The only pollution we can hope to prevent is that within our own spirits, with the grace of the Holy Spirit. The only pollution we can hope to prevent is hardness and coldness within our own hearts; it was meanness of spirit, hardness and coldness of heart that most troubled Jesus, and we have to watch out for it, make sure that as Christians we do not behave like the pharisee but like the publican.

And we must remember that God has given us a beautiful planet in a beautiful solar system in a beautiful galaxy in a beautiful universe, and we human beings have been created to be beautiful, too, with loving, compassionate hearts.

And I think of my teenaged granddaughters and their friends, and I have hope for this world, because they are thoughtful and joyful and willing to share and to work with courage and grace.

Martin E. Marty
Historian, Theologian

He is Distinguished Service Professor, University of Chicago Divinity School and an award-winning author of some forty books. He is the Senior Editor of The Christian Century.

N ever in my life has a young person come up to this veteran of almost six decades of life and asked, "What advice would you give me as I look forward to adulthood?" I doubt whether many of you ever have directly asked such a question. That does not mean that it is a bad one. It simply is a form of language few of us find easy to use. The young feel uncomfortable asking, and their seniors fear that they will sound condescending if they try to answer.

If the question never comes directly, it can and does come indirectly and often. Younger people ask it of older people simply by keeping their eyes open, watching how people they admire or are curious about live their lives. They read book-length biographies or magazine-length sketches of celebrities, heroines, saints, exemplars. Or they find words, but these words don't quite match the formal question. "Dad, I don't see why you don't ever . . . " "Mom, can you ever remember a time when you . . . ?" "Teacher, I wonder why at this point in your career and my studies you . . ." "Can you remember back when you . . . ?" And the older, asked, person, probably mumbles back little half answers that, in the course of long conversations, add up to whole philosophies of life. By the way, the older partner in conversation may also be asking such questions of the young, hoping to learn something that will keep him or her fresh and full of spiritual and moral energies.

One way to answer the big question is to picture what others ask when they size up a person who has evolved into an adult. My no-frills answer sets up one such scene.

Here it is: My advice to you is that you develop, or let develop, your "core."

Now the incident. A university president wanted me to recommend a certain person to him who could serve as a dean. I described a good candidate, telling of all this person's competences, skills, and experiences. It all sounded good. Then the president snapped a question, "Has this person a 'core'?" It came with stunning directness and I, unprepared, had an immediate answer: "Yes, that's the most obvious and important thing . . . "

Often, since then, I have thought about the question and the answer. I came home and looked up *core* in the dictionary. I read of apple cores and electrical cores, and then came upon this: "The central or innermost part, the 'heart' of anything." Or anyone. It also occurred to me that the English core is a pun on the Latin *cor,* or "heart." You have to have a "heart."

Whatever can all this mean? I think I know what was in the question, and I know what I put into the answer. Some people go through life without a core. Some are good blotters, who soak up what others have left. Others are good antennae, who get their signals from whatever is in the air. Still other people are good mirrors, who bounce back whatever anyone around beams their way. Such people can become quick and flashy and glib. They can make good impressions. They have an answer for everything, a quip or a suggestion for any situation. Yet if they lack a core, a center to their existence, this will in due course show up. They won't wear well. In Peter de Vries' terms about such a person, "on the surface she's profound, but way down deep she's superficial."

People advised to develop a core must begin by recognizing themselves as distinct creations of God. You are one of a kind, with distinctive gifts, unique experiences. You are a social being, dependent on others for survival at first, and connected with others all your life. You accept the gifts of goodness from some social beings around you, and you reject menaces. You are a critical person, armed with an intelligence that lets you appraise others and yourself.

You are to be a responsible being, who takes your special place among others.

Gradually your core develops. People find that you have and express a center. For the Christian this means that you have found your life "hid with Christ in God." Thus you are rooted, not likely to be blown away with every breeze and drift. You have Christ as model, for in his love and courage you see the perfect instance of someone with a core, a heart.

As yours develops, you'll have to sort out many philosophies. Chances are, yours will grow most deeply when you suffer and have setbacks, since a person with a core will not let failure lead to despair any more than she will let success lead to pride. You will have to turn the mirror on yourself without becoming a narcissist, to seek, as the Greeks urged, to "know thyself" without getting all wrapped up in yourself. If friends come to you for counsel, if people you hardly know start trusting you, you will know that your "core"—your true self—is developing.

It has to keep developing. There's no stage at which you can allow it to harden, to become too well defined. It's the dynamic heart of you, always in need of growing, always seeking models and finding the best in the Model of our ways as well as our grace-full enabler, Jesus Christ.

Malcolm Thomas Muggeridge
Journalist, Social Critic

Known for his sharp humor, he is internationally recognized as one of the twentieth century's most insightful observers. In addition to his lifetime of news writing, he has written novels, plays, biographies, and hundreds of book reviews. He was an outspoken atheist for most of his life; he became a Christian in his later years and has written best-selling books on Christianity.

Young people must, I think, begin with the recognition that the Word has come among us. The indescribable fact that Jesus, the Word made flesh, has entered human history is where meaning begins. Scripture and human history are replete with examples of godly men and women who by their lives help us to find real Truth.

I am concerned that modern education excludes any teaching of Christian values. Young people are taught that power—technological, scientific, political—can provide humans with a prosperous and better world and a contented life. They are encouraged to believe that we can create a perfect society, or if not perfect, vastly improved. This is a complete fallacy. Solutions will never come from human efforts. History has demonstrated this again and again.

I have said many times that media are vehicles of fantasy, especially television. Young people need to be very cautious about television because television will subject them to very unpleasant things—to corrupting values in advertising and in the programs. As much as possible they should walk away from being subjected to debauchery.

In addition, teachers and counselors who are advising young people—guiding in the spiritual sense of Bunyan's *Pilgrim's Progress*—in nine cases out of ten today, never hold out to young people the challenge of a Christian life. There is a loss of the sense of moral order in the universe. Here is where the examples of godly men and women, in Scripture, in biographies and in present-day saints like Mother Teresa, can be extremely useful.

Very simply, I would say to young people, read the Gospels, follow Christ's way, and whatever the twenty-first century brings, everything will be all right.

Alan Paton
Novelist

After the publication of his first book, Cry, the Beloved Country, *he became active in the political life of South Africa. He was a devoted leader in the struggle to end the oppression of Blacks in his country. An Anglican layman, Paton's Christian faith illuminated his lifelong efforts to further justice and peace. Alan Paton died in 1988; this is one of the last pieces he wrote.*

*T*his is not the first time that I have presumed to give advice to persons younger than myself. I am often asked to speak at schools on their prize days or on the occasion which in America is called "commencement," and I assume that I am expected to say a special word to those who are leaving school and who are "going out into the world." Sometimes the young people come to see me themselves, to ask for advice on some problem that faces them, and naturally I try to respond to them, though not always in the way that they expect, as I shall later explain.

What do I say when I speak at a commencement? I first tell them a story that they all know already, and that is the story of the Washing of the Feet.

So when He had washed their feet, taken His garments, and sat down again, He said to them, "Do you know what I have done to you? You call me teacher and Lord, and you say well, for so I am. If I then, your Lord and teacher have washed your feet, you also ought to wash one another's feet. If you know these things, happy are you if you do them." (John 13:12-17 NKJV)

And then I repeat those final words: "If you know these things, happy are you if you do them."

I tell my young listeners that these are not only religious words, suitable especially for church and Sundays. They are true always; they tell one of the deepest truths about human life. If you know these things, and you don't do them, then your life can never be happy. If you know these things, and you do them, then that will give you a happiness that cannot be taken away. This is not a promise that if you use your life to serve others, you will never know any unhappiness, or will never experience loss or pain. I close my address by telling my listeners that my greatest wish for them is not that they will have a happy life, though I do wish that for them also, but rather that they will find a worthwhile purpose for their lives, a purpose for living. Much of the unhappiness in the world is to be found among people who either have no purpose for their lives, or who don't believe that there is any purpose in life at all. If one believes that, it is an easy step to a life of drugs and uselessness, and to the endless pursuit of pleasures that bring no joy.

I wrote earlier that when young people come to me for advice, I try to respond, though not always in the way that they expect, and I shall give you an example. When young people ask for advice as to whether they should take a course of action that may have painful consequences for themselves, I tell them that I cannot advise them, and that in fact it would be wrong for me to do so. A young white man asks me whether he should refuse to do military service, because he believes that would mean taking up arms against black people either on the border or in some restless black township. If he refuses to do his service, he may be punished, either by confinement to barracks or by having to do hospital or some other non-combatant work. Some of these young men will also refuse to do any non-combatant work, thus laying themselves open to criminal charges and possibly imprisonment. I tell them they must decide for themselves. When I was their age, I had to make my own decisions on difficult problems such as these.

I encourage young people who feel it to be their duty to fight against injustice in their society, but I tell them they must not be obsessed by injustice. There is nothing in the world by which one should become obsessed. The very word "obsession" carries the implication of an unnatural and unhealthy state of mind. One not only has a duty to others, one has a duty to oneself as well. And indeed, if one neglects one's duty to oneself, one is unable to do one's duty to others as well as one could. There are some people who believe that one has no right to happiness so long as there is unhappiness in the world. I do not believe it.

We are taught that it is right "to have life more abundantly." We have a right to enjoy it, so long as we remember the needs of others. We must never lose our sense of humor. Humor is a gift that prevents one from taking life too seriously. Look at the face of Mother Teresa. She has taken life seriously, but she has not lost her humanity and her kindness. When duty makes you unkind—and I know people whom duty had made unkind—then obviously you are becoming obsessed by it.

If you know these things, happy are you if you do them.

John Paul II (Karol Wojtyla)
Pope

He was a professor of moral theology at the University of Krakow and University of Lublin. Writing for many years under the pen name Andrzej Jawien, he published several volumes of poetry and a play. He served as Archbishop of Krakow and as a Roman Catholic cardinal before he was elected Pope in 1978.

*L*ove is essential. This theme places before our eyes the witness of the apostle St. John, when he exclaims: "We ourselves have known and put our faith in God's love toward ourselves" (I John 4:16).

Since we can neither live nor understand ourselves without love, I want to appeal to you to grow in humanity, to give absolute priority to the values of the spirit, and to transform yourselves into "new persons" by increasingly recognizing and accepting the presence of God in your life; the presence of a God who is Love; of a Father who loves each one of us for the whole of eternity, who created us by love, and who loved us so much that he gave up his only Son to forgive us of our sins, to reconcile us to him, and to enable us to live with him in a communion of love that will never end.

The world anxiously awaits our witness of life, a witness born from a deep personal conviction and a sincere act of love and faith in the Risen Christ. This is what is meant by experiencing love and believing in it.

There is an inescapable need of the love of God and the communion of those who feel themselves to be children of the same Father, brothers and sisters in Jesus Christ, and united by the power of the Spirit. By forming part of the great family of the redeemed and by being living members of the Church, you will experience the enthusiasm and joy of the love of God by which you are called to unity and solidarity. This is a call that excludes no one. On the contrary, it is one that transcends frontiers and is addressed to all young people without distinction. It is a call that strengthens and renews the bonds by which young people are united. In these conditions, it is essential that the bonds that unite them be particularly strong and operative with the young who are suffering from unemployment, who are living in poverty or solitude, who feel themselves marginalized, or who bear the heavy cross of sickness.

It is essential, too, that this message of friendship also reach those who do not accept religious faith. Charity does not compromise with error, but it goes out toward everyone to open up the paths to conversion. How splendid and luminous are the words addressed to us in this respect by St. Paul in his hymn to charity! (I Corinthians 13). May they be for you a program of conduct and resolute commitment for your present and future life!

The love of God poured into our hearts by the Holy Spirit must deepen our awareness of the blatant threats posed by hunger and war, the scandalous disparities between opulent minorities and poor peoples, the violations of human rights and fundamental human liberties, including the right to religious freedom, and actual or potential manipulations of dignity.

More than ever, it is vitally important that the enormous scientific and technological advances of our time be directed, with moral wisdom, to the well-being of the whole of humanity. The gravity, urgency, and complexity of current problems and challenges demand of the new generations the necessary capacity and competence in the various fields, but the integral well-being of humanity, created in the image of God and called to an eternal destiny, must be placed above partial interests and viewpoints.

It is in Christ that the love of God and the sublime dignity of human beings have been fully revealed to us. May Jesus be the "cornerstone" of your life and of the new civilization you are called to build in a spirit of generous solidarity and sharing. No authentic human growth in peace and justice, in truth and freedom, can be achieved without the presence of Christ and his salvific power.

The building of a civilization of love requires strong

and persevering character, ready for self-sacrifice and anxious to open up new paths of human coexistence by overcoming divisions and the various forms of materialism. This is a responsibility of the young people of today who will be the men and women of tomorrow, at the dawn of the third Christian millennium.

Start out on the road! May your journey be marked by prayer, study, dialogue, and the desire for conversion and a better life. Go forward united with one another in your parishes and Christian communities. May yours be an attitude of acceptance and hope.

I send my cordial greetings to all the young people of the world.

Dear young people, my friends: be witnesses to the love of God, sowers of hope and builders of peace.

In the name of the Lord Jesus, I bless you with all my affection.

From an address on the World Day of Youth, Palm Sunday, 1987, Buenos Aires, Argentina.

Wesley G. Pippert
Journalist

Director of Washington Graduate Program, University of Missouri School of Journalism. As a Washington journalist he covered Watergate, the McGovern and Carter presidential campaigns, and the Ford and Carter presidencies for United Press International. He was a senior foreign correspondent in Israel and the Middle East.

*A*s you look forward to adulthood, I would say, simply: Be curious; be disciplined. And above all, don't forget two important loves: Love God; love others.

Curiosity helps us overcome whatever deficiencies we feel we may have experienced as children. Curiosity helps keep us young by continually exposing us to new things. Be curious about just about everything. About cities, about the countryside. About books, about nature. About sports, about the arts. About politics, about interior decorating and architecture. Not all of us will experience love in marriage. In my own case I was a single adult for a long time and often felt that I probably would never marry. In some ways, the single person is able to investigate and do more things than a married person or a parent restricted by the demands of home and family.

I'm interested in everything—at first I probably had to teach myself to be interested in everything, and now I'm curious enough that I don't know whether I'm interested in something because I taught myself to be or whether my interest was sparked spontaneously! I have at least a dozen mini-collections—of each new U.S. stamp that has been released annually for the past 15 years; of dollar bills bearing the signature of every secretary of the treasury and U.S. treasurer since Franklin D. Roosevelt was president, of letters and envelopes with the uncounted ways my name has been misspelled, of maps old and new.

Here are some of the things (that became an important part of my life) I did for the first time as an adult:

—Water-skied for the first time at age 25.

—Traveled abroad for the first time at age 29.

—Got my master's degree at age 32.

—Went deep-sea fishing for the first time at age 34.

—Snow-skied for the first time at age 35.

—Cultivated an interest in the arts, especially painting, architecture, and concert music, in my 30s.

—Got married at age 43.

—Uprooted our home and left the city I had lived in for sixteen years to start living abroad at age 49.

—Became a father for the first time at age 50.

—And, importantly, took regular sabbaticals to get away from routine and to allow for probing new things and ideas. I have had four sabbaticals, almost all of them a year in length.

In other words, a person is never too old to learn or do something new.

Curiosity, however, needs to be disciplined in order to avoid the danger of simply acting with license and abandon. One of the most effective disciplines I know is not to do something that first time—for repetition will come far easier. Avoid that first drink, that first smoke, that first taste of sexual immorality, that first drug. Not doing something the first time is a tremendous bulwark against not doing it later. As moral philosopher Sissela Bok has said in her book, *Lying* (New York: Pantheon, 1978, p. 25), "It is easy to tell a lie but hard to tell only one." Discipline will help us avoid the guilt that we often experience by dabbling in things we shouldn't.

An important fruit of discipline is integrity. Few things are more important than whether one has a good reputation, a "good name." Not all people are gregarious or outgoing. Not all people are sought after or "loveable." But everyone can have integrity. Integrity flows more out of a disciplined character than a dashing personality.

Finally, and perhaps most important of all, don't forget the gift of love. All of us, young and old, ought to love God and love others. This is the greatest mark of a person, whether that person is young or old, rich or poor, impoverished or affluent.

C. William Pollard

Businessman

He is chairman and chief executive officer of ServiceMaster Industries, an international service company, and serves on the boards of many business and ministry oranizations.

E very one of us needs values—a group of beliefs and absolutes that govern our basic actions. This is especially true in today's world when we are encouraged to believe that we live only for the moment.

I think it is of particular importance that any discussion of values be based on the one absolute that still exists in our chaotic world: the Word of God. By starting with God as the Ultimate Source rather than with the world, we recognize that our values extend beyond the limits of time, geography, and society.

A God-based value system infiltrates and controls every area of our lives. It unifies our relationships with our family, our peers, our friends, and our work associates. We cannot have one value system for home and church, and another for work.

As you make the transition from a life spent mostly in school to one spent primarily at work, you will discover even more the importance of basing your value system on the teaching of Scripture.

Unfortunately for many in the business world, the only value is the one expressed in the dollar bill. But there are companies and organizations whose values go beyond that of money. At the company I work for, our first objective is "To honor God in all we do."

This is not simply an expression of a denominational belief or the advocacy of the free-enterprise system wrapped in a religious blanket. It is an affirmative statement that says a business's source and starting point can be with God. Because of this starting point, a personal value system can develop, influencing how workers live with themselves, with others, and with their families. It recognizes that there are God-given standards, God-given limitations, and God-given freedoms that can be used in relationships, in decisions, and in every aspect of life.

Let me share with you some specific applications.

First of all, God recognizes your value as a person. You are created in God's image and have a responsibility and accountability to your Creator for yourself and for others. Every single person has been created with dignity and intrinsic worth. The idea that your value as an individual should be related to your income or wealth is wholly repugnant to the Christian view of the human person.

It is not enough to say that a company is moral or ethical if it determines a worker's fair wage and pays it. This thinking is humanistic in its origin. When this type of thinking is combined with the emphasis on making a profit in a free-enterprise system, the result is often the search for an alternative to people. People are viewed as the most costly and unreliable part of the work process. A company seeking to honor God will value you as a person, not seek an alternative to you. It will train and motivate you to be more effective so that you will receive the satisfaction of a job well done. A person with a purpose to serve provides an element of dependability and response far greater than any machine.

A company that honors God looks beyond the value of the individual to the value of the family. The family is the basic spiritual, economic, and social unit for your development. A business needs to be concerned about employees' families and lives outside of the workplace. This concern focuses on the future importance of relating to the needs of your spouse and your children, if God blesses you in these ways.

God has provided work as a vehicle for you to learn and to grow as well as to provide for your human needs. Work can be a calling and a ministry to God and to a person's development. In the Christian view, work is never just a job, a way to earn a living, or a way-station until retirement. This recognition should be woven into your values.

Another consideration involves covenants and commitments as a basis for team effort in the place of business. God established the use of the covenant as a means of initiating and ensuring cooperative action and joint response from his people. A company seeking to honor God can only have a collective ministry because there are covenants and commitments of managers with each other. This is more than merely a written employment contract. When a manager leads you, for example, it is in the spirit of developing you to be ready for whatever future opportunities may lie ahead.

The last value has to do with economics. It is the value of produced wealth that should be invested as it is earned and not retained for personal interests. The principle here is that the wealth that God has provided is only held in trust by you. You are not the actual owner; God is. So as a steward, you are to use it, to invest it, to enjoy it, but not to dissipate or waste it.

These five values, the worth of the individual, of the family, of work, of commitments, and of invested resources can provide your life with lasting meaning. They will stand you in excellent stead in whatever career you enter. I am excited about the tremendous potential before you. You can share in the vision for that potential. May your own value system provide you with the basis for directing you through the challenges and opportunities of the future.

Kenneth Taylor
Bible Translator, Publisher

His best-known work is The Living Bible, *a modern biblical paraphrase which is in thirteen foreign versions.* The Living New Testament *paraphrase is in fifty-five languages. He is founder and president of Tyndale Publishers and Living Bibles International.*

Your life contains a precious cargo of good things of God to be given to others. You are going out into a world of wild waves and hidden rocks and reefs, in an unmarked channel. You have never been there before, and you will never be there again. Who is at the helm? Is it you? I hope not. I counsel you to turn your life over to God who has offered to take the helm for you. He knows every step of the way, and he will bring you safely to the port of his desire—the place where he has purposed for you to be, accomplishing all that he has planned for you from before the founding of the world.

Now let me change the scene. You are, in a sense, at the bottom rung of a ladder leaning up against a tall building. In fact, there are many tall buildings with ladders. Each building is plainly marked. One of them says "Wealth" and another "Popularity," and another "The Good Things of This Life." Step by step you will climb through the years to the goal of your choice, and you will probably arrive at your destination. But if you start climbing any of the buildings except the one marked, "The Will of God," you will spend your life in a long, hard, frustrating climb, and in the end you will find yourself on the top of the wrong building.

My urgent advice, then, is to choose the will of God for your life, and ask him to keep you steadily on course toward that goal.

There are ways to get strength and wisdom for the life ahead. One of these is the practice of regular Bible reading. I recommend this on a daily basis because I believe it is God's Word and, therefore, the most important book in the world. The time to get into this habit is now, at the beginning of the journey, rather than "when all else fails, read the instructions!" Get into the habit of reading God's Word as a young person, asking God to stimulate your thinking, and to give you joy and peace and power for accomplishing the good things he wants you to do.

Don't forget, too, that prayer is exceedingly important. For whatever reason, God has arranged that some of the things he wants to do, he does only when we have prayed. Some of the things he would like to do, he cannot do in and through our lives because we don't spend time with him in prayer.

So ask God to take charge of your life, and then you do your part by reading his Word and speaking with him on a regular basis.

Ruth Welting

Opera Singer

She has sung leading roles at the New York City Opera, Metropolitan Opera, Chicago Lyric Opera, Royal Opera House Covent Garden, Paris, Netherlands, and Buenos Aires Operas. She has been a soloist with the Chicago, Philadelphia, and San Francisco Symphony Orchestras.

*T*he advice I would give you as you look forward to adulthood is that you not enter it alone. Take Jesus Christ with you.

The first twenty-seven years of my life I struggled with myself and the world around me. Although I had achieved quite a lot in terms of the world's success, in the end, I found it all worthless. To step on and over people in the name of selfish ambition leaves you empty, even if it works. Sin only leaves you needing more, whether that sin is worshiping at the shrine of music, or worshiping anything other than God. The name doesn't matter; the result is the same.

What is it like to be a surrendered life in opera? What is it like to take Jesus with you onstage? Everything changes for the artist. You no longer sing to gain people's approval. You no longer strive to exalt self and career. You have substituted yourself for Jesus and his career. Your gifts become beautiful hooks on the ends of God-controlled lines. You are now fishers of people.

Sometimes people may be offended that you, as an artist, refuse to be an idol. Yet you sense your light burning brighter, even as people try to obscure it with the bushel basket of Matthew 5:15.

In a secular field, you need a Christian support system. Proverbs 27:17 says, "Iron sharpens iron." That is what Christian friends can do. Without them you can't keep aware of the pitfalls of Satan and still be used by God. God will send you Christian support as you ask him.

As a youth in Italy, I sang for a very famous group of musicians who all told me I had talent. Yet one of them said: "Don't pursue a career in the arts unless you have to!" He meant that the price of excellence is high, and mediocrity is plentiful.

There are a lot of ways to prove God through faith. One is in the naked truth of performing. Almost all opera singers are afraid of audiences. Facing an audience's acceptance or rejection is a reality after each performance. The audience is not always honest and not always fair. As a Christian, I have the promises of God as a covering for my fears. He will never let the righteous be ashamed; he has never failed me. Perfect love casts out fear. At least it has for me.

Music is a gift and a tool. I have learned that we

must never see it as more than it is. If I accept music as from God, if I perform through God offering my singing to God, I can keep it all in perspective.

Many younger and older people tell me, "I do not want to turn over my life to Jesus because he will take away my music or my career." People always seem to believe God takes things away. He didn't take away my career. Why should he take away yours? We sometimes forget that God is the one who gave us our gift in the first place. He only takes away those things that hurt us.

Salvation in Christ will never rob you of anything, and with God, life is never boring. There is a great plan for your life. There is a freedom from ego and the burdens life puts on us. Obeying God gives freedom, and the highest freedom we can know is in the framework of discipline; discipline yourself through God.

Christians in the performing arts know that the only truly unique gift comes through God's anointing on that gift. It is in becoming God's son or daughter, and as he touches us, we become stars and lights.

David Winter

Television Producer, Writer, Minister

A distinguished British Broadcasting Corporation producer, writer of many books on Christian life, he recently left the BBC to minister as a vicar in a parish church near Oxford, England.

I've been given a great deal of advice in my life. Probably to my cost, I've ignored most of it, but there are things I've been told that I've remembered and acted on, and that have helped me to cope with various situations that inevitably crop up. I'm almost as bad at giving advice as following it, but perhaps I can combine the two by passing on to you some of it that has been of help to me.

The first, and most fundamental, is to "stick to principles." I remember thinking, when a minister I greatly admired said it to me, that that was all right in theory, but in practice "principles" could be a bit of a luxury. But over the years I've proved to my own satisfaction that it is not only theoretically right—and ethically and morally sound—but it actually *works*.

Once you abandon principles and start to play for popularity or success or ends, you are lost in a jungle. There are no direction signs, no lights, no route-maps. You've decided to leave the beaten path and the known way, and one fatal step will bring disaster.

I don't say I've always followed the advice, but I can say disregarding it has always brought catastrophe. If your principles—*Christian* principles, I hope—tell you that a certain course of action is wrong, however desirable the result that it is supposed to bring about, then follow the principles. At least that way you know why you are doing it. At least you can live with yourself.

Often in the world of the media there is a temptation to abandon or compromise principles. It may be a tempting shortcut to popularity. It may be a way to achieve instant notoriety—by broadcasting innuendoes or rumors about a public figure, perhaps, or by stoking up controversy or anger in a talk show. It may involve abandoning truthfulness or integrity or loyalty.

If principles become the casualties of your pragmatism—prices you are prepared to pay in pursuit of your ambition—then, beware! As Paul says, "Sin pays its servants. The salary is *death*." Those who cast aside loyalty can't expect others to be loyal to them. Those who tell lies cannot expect to learn the truth. Those who compromise integrity will find that, in the end, nobody trusts them.

So—"stick to your principles" is good, sound advice. It's right, and it works.

The second piece of advice I have remembered, and

tried to act on, is "Be anxious about nothing." It's a saying of Paul's from the Letter to the Philippians, and I've had more trouble with this one, because I have a vivid imagination, and that is often the fuel of anxiety. I can easily imagine awful things happening to those I love, terrible complications and disruptions to the even, smooth process of my life. I'm not, in the ordinary sense of the word, a "worrier," but I can get consumed with anxiety.

Now the advice "Be anxious about nothing" is obviously good advice, but—once again—is it practical? Someone quite recently pointed out to me ninety percent of what we worry about *never happens,* so we have wasted all that nervous energy worrying about . . . what? *Nothing.*

We worry the plane might crash. It doesn't. We worry the kids will get on drugs. They don't. We worry that we will lose our job and we'll be made obsolete. We don't and we aren't. We worry that if we're late getting home no one else will start dinner. We are, but they do. All day long we're burdened with big or small anxieties—anything from a spoiled meal to a plane crash—and most of it never happens.

So, what is the answer? Here's the third piece of advice, given me soon after I became a Christian: "Take it to the Lord in prayer." Turn anxieties into intercessions. Turn your vivid imagination into believing prayer. Hand it over to God. "Be anxious about nothing, but in *everything,* by prayer with thanksgiving, make your requests known to God."

Let him take the burden, as he has offered to do. Leave it with him.

The fourth piece of advice I was given, and have tried to follow, is "Aim high." If we set ourselves small goals, we'll achieve small results. The Bible is full of enormous goals set by God and Jesus for their followers: Be perfect (Matthew 5:48). Evangelize the whole world (Matthew 28:19). Love your enemies (Matthew 5:44). Transform your minds (Romans 12:2). Turn the world upside down (Acts 17:6). Heal the sick (Matthew 10:8). Pursue peace (Romans 12:18). Be salt and light for all the world (Matthew 5:13-14).

Humility is a virtue, but lack of vision is a sin. The world is full of people asking small things of a small God. As J. B. Phillips wrote, "Your God is too small." I think of the Hindu intellectual who said of the Christians he had met that they seemed to be "very ordinary people making extraordinary claims." In one way, he was right—but those "claims" must be put to the test. I prefer the great missionary slogan, "Attempt great things for God, expect great things from God." Those who expect little will receive little: "What you sow, you reap." The person who sows sparingly will reap sparingly (Galatians 6:7).

You have, God willing, a whole life ahead of you. Don't waste it. Don't arrive at fifty or sixty years of age asking where it all went, and what have you achieved. Set yourself some goals. Stick to your principles. And *don't worry*.